HOW TO CHOOSE THE RIGHT MANAGEMENT COMPANY FOR YOUR RESIDENTIAL PROPERTY

A DECISION-MAKER'S GUIDE

BY
LESLIE KAMINOFF, *RAM, *NYARM
AND
BARBARA DERSHOWITZ

*Registered Apartment Manager
*New York Accredited Realty Manager

bdci publishing
& communications

Long Island, New York

HOW TO CHOOSE
THE RIGHT
MANAGEMENT COMPANY
FOR YOUR RESIDENTIAL PROPERTY
A DECISION-MAKER'S GUIDE

First Edition / First Printing September 1995.
Printed in the United States of America.

ISBN: 0-9647619-0-4
Library of Congress Catalog Card Number: 95-78374

Published by bdci
423 Jericho Turnpike
Suite 136
Syosset, New York   11791

For mail orders/inquiries, see **Special Offers** on page 85, or write:
bdci, 423 Jericho Turnpike, Suite 136, Syosset, NY 11791

PLEASE NOTE: The authors believe all information contained in this work to be factual and accurate. However, laws, regulations, and industry standards change constantly. Readers are advised to consult appropriate legal and/or other counsel before taking any action based on the information contained herein. This publication should not be used as a substitute for appropriate professional counsel.

DEDICATION

This book is dedicated with love to

Kim, Alexis, Ashley, and Justin

and

Steve, Adam, and Lauren

Whose patience and understanding allow us to do our work at all hours of the day and night, and still return to the place we love best: Home.

And to You,

The Property Decision-Maker,

With the sincere hope that we have provided valuable, practical, and useful information that will help you meet your challenges and make your life easier.

CONTENTS

FOREWORD

Caveat Emptor – Let the buyer beware. An important maxim to live by under any circumstances, but especially true when selecting appropriate management for your residential property.

The field of residential property management has come a long way since people began living in communal environments. Whereas once, the laws governing multi-unit dwellings were relatively simple and straightforward, and the landlord was keeper of the gates, personally responsible for everything that went on in his property, today the residential landscape is vastly different.

New rules and regulations of governance and taxation, new systems of internal operation, and new issues surrounding shared responsibility all have contributed to the evolution of the residential property management field, which has burgeoned over the past two decades, especially in urban and suburban areas.

The industry has evolved into one that demands ever-increasing specialized knowledge, skills, and professionalism to keep pace with advances in technology, with new and constantly changing legislation, and with the rapid emergence of cooperatives, condominiums, and homeowners associations (HOAs) throughout the country.

In densely-populated cities, for example, where developers respond to the scarcity of land by building upward, communal ownership of multi-unit dwellings is now available on the same lot where once only a single-family home would have stood. In the forms of cooperatives and condominiums, these vertical neighborhoods have given rise to the unique need for the specific services offered only by professional management.

Outside the cities, foresightful developers have created self-sustaining mini-communities, characterized either by attractive attached or semi-attached housing units, or by custom-built homes on spacious lots, as in the case of homeowners associations. Owners in both types of communities invest not only in their own living space proper, but also in the privilege of participating in such shared amenities and services as common recreational facilities, common grounds caretaking, and, of course, essential common management to oversee it all.

The challenge is real for the rental property owner/landlord, the developer/sponsor, and the cooperative, condominium, or HOA Board seeking new management. Charged with making a decision that will inevitably have far-reaching financial, structural, and quality-of-life consequences, these individuals must take seriously the task of identifying and engaging the most qualified, most appropriate management for their properties.

Moreover, the process of management selection is, as anyone who has ever done it will attest, both complicated and time-consuming. But its reward is also real. Done well, the selection process can be smooth, and yield a lasting association between property and management that saves time and money, enhances the value of the property, and protects the investments of those who share in its ownership.

With this in mind, prudent property decision-makers will embrace the wisdom of educating themselves about their management options as best they can immediately upon the decision to seek new management. And the book you are reading now is an invaluable resource for just that kind of education.

Complete, informative, and accessibly well-written, *How to Choose the Right Management Company for Your Residential Property: A Decision-Maker's Guide* is the product of experience no theory can replace. Few professionals bring to the table greater familiarity with the intricacies of residential property management than the authors of this book. Readers are well-advised to consider strongly every valuable suggestion made on these pages.

Even property decision-makers with management already in place will benefit from this book, since it clearly and succinctly defines the services good management should provide, and the nature of a productive property/management relationship.

That said, I'm pleased to have my name associated with this fine effort.

With all best wishes for a successful management search,

Albert Greenbaum
President
Municipal Data Services, Inc.
Real Estate Consultant

INTRODUCTION

As a decision-maker for your property, you know first-hand the complex responsibilities involved in operating a successful, financially viable multi-unit residential environment.

From ensuring structural integrity to creating and working within a budget of several hundred thousand – perhaps millions – of dollars, the obligations you have assumed, and the decisions you make, have a lasting impact on your property's value and quality-of-life.

If yours is like the overwhelming majority of rental properties, cooperatives, condominiums, and townehouse/home-owners associations throughout the United States, you rely on the services of an independent professional residential management organization for the daily, short-, and long-term operation of your investment. Engaging the right management company is arguably the most important decision you and your colleague decision-makers will make.

As experience no doubt has informed you, the residential management arena is populated by a wide range of companies, and finding the right one for your property is challenging. Knowing the right questions to ask, and how to interpret the volumes of information generated by a management search, will enable you to choose the management company that can best provide the knowledgeable, responsive, accessible, and honest service your property needs.

This book will help you and your decision-making colleagues become more aware of your management options. It will educate you about how management companies operate, and provide a basis for comparison so that you can make the right decision – a decision that will stand the test of time, that will help your property achieve its maximum value, and that will identify your property as an outstanding place in which to live.

Engaging the right management company is arguably the most important decision you and your colleague decision-makers will make... Knowing the right questions to ask, and how to interpret the volumes of information generated by a management search, will enable you to choose the management company that can best provide the knowledgeable, responsive, accessible, and honest service your property needs.

ONE:

WHAT YOU NEED TO KNOW ABOUT PROFESSIONAL RESIDENTIAL MANAGEMENT

Owners of multi-unit residential properties are responsible for the management of their properties. In a rental building, for example, the responsibility and accountability fall to the landlord/owner. In cooperatives, condominiums, and townehouse/homeowners associations (HOAs), management responsibility falls to the individuals who own the property communally. In co-ops, it's the shareholders. In condos, it's the unit owners. And in townehouse/homeowners associations, it's the homeowners.

The management of any residential property – whether it's a single, multi-unit building, a complex of multi-unit buildings, or a series of detached single family homes within an association – is a formidable and time-consuming activity. It includes everything from collecting maintenance, common charges, and/or rent, to making certain that the boiler functions properly, to complying with local codes, ordinances, laws, and regulations. It requires 24-hour-a-day, seven-day-a-week attention, and round-the-clock availability to handle emergencies whenever they occur. It is, in short, a full-time job.

The professional residential management industry has evolved to provide daily and ongoing management services to owners who are themselves unable to devote round-the-clock attention and supervision to their properties. Landlords/owners, developers/sponsors/converters, and democratically-elected owner representatives in the forms of Boards of Directors, Boards of Managers, and Association Boards, engage professional residential management companies to implement their decisions and policies, and to help identify and facilitate the immediate, short-, and long-term goals of their properties.

> *Owners of multi-unit residential properties are responsible for the management of their properties... The management of any residential property ... is a formidable and time-consuming activity... It requires 24-hour-a-day, seven-day-a-week attention ... It is, in short, a full-time job.*

What a Professional Management Company Does

Ideally, the residential management company you engage for your property will be involved, under your direction, with every aspect of your property's operation.

(4)

Most management companies claim to offer the same basic services in exchange for a contract fee, usually payable on a monthly basis. But beware: All management companies are *not* the same.

A full-service residential management company should be equipped to:

- Be responsible for the ongoing maintenance of your property, including its structural integrity and buildingwide systems (including but not limited to the facade, boilers and burners, energy, elevators, security, the roof, windows, laundry facilities, pool, etc.)
- Establish, oversee, and implement effective preventive maintenance programs
- Supervise, hire, and fire staff; and create and manage job descriptions, work schedules, and staff performance
- Oversee finances, including but not limited to the billing and collection of maintenance/common charges/rent; payment of vendor/contractor and utility bills; payment of mortgage, taxes, and other obligations
- Provide accurate financial statements on a regular basis; and assist with contract negotiations, purchasing, and the creation and implementation of annual and long-term operations and special budgets
- Distribute salaries to your property's staff
- Receive, interpret, and respond appropriately to

violations; and to federal, state, and local laws and regulations governing your type of living environment

- Establish and maintain an accurate inventory tracking system
- Maintain accurate, accessible files, records, and financial books for your property
- Offer and provide capital project planning and management assistance
- Prepare for and attend regular and special Board meetings; and promulgate timely notice for, and attend, annual and special meetings of your property's owners
- Interact knowledgeably and effectively with your property's other professionals, including legal counsel, accountants, engineers, architects, and others
- Respond courteously, timely, and effectively to resident inquiries and concerns; and disseminate information to residents according to your instruction.

You and your decision-making colleagues should review the services listed above with an eye to your own property. You should determine the level and types of services your property needs, wants, and can afford, and then seek out those companies with proven histories of providing those services.

Many management companies offer additional services, such as mortgage brokerage, and sales and rental brokerage, usually for additional fees. A company that quotes an attractively low management fee may expect to make up the difference through your property's use of its ancillary services, and you should bear this in mind when considering a new management company.

> *Most management companies claim to offer the same basic services in exchange for a contract fee... But beware: All management companies are not the same.*

The Spectrum of Management Companies

Although most professional residential management companies claim to offer similar services, every company is unique in terms of age, size, expertise, and philosophy. To choose the right management company for your property, you'll want to consider all aspects of a company's operation.

While there are exceptions, experience has shown the following to be true.

Large management companies typically manage a portfolio of 100 or more properties. Most large companies have been in business for many years, and are self-contained; they employ

(7)

the personnel and own the technology that allow them to offer the most extensive service menu and to provide most services in-house. In general, larger management organizations may provide a higher level of experience than their smaller counterparts, and greater economy of scale when it comes to such services as banking, purchasing supplies, etc.

(For example, larger management organizations are in a position to make favorable bulk purchasing arrangements with distributors and suppliers of commonly-used services and products. A larger management company may be able to invite your property to participate in a reduced-rate arrangement with a fuel company, for instance, based on the volume of business the management firm does with that fuel company. Of course, your property should be under no obligation to purchase from that particular fuel supplier when you choose to engage that management organization.)

In terms of personnel advantage, a larger management company usually can provide better coverage and back-up for your property when your site professional/managing agent is not in the office or is on vacation or extended sick leave. The concern that your property will be lost in the crowd when you work with a large management organization may be legitimate; however, such a company's ability to assign existing internal personnel to your property at a moment's notice is a strong advantage to counterbalance this concern.

You also should be able to expect greater access to a wider variety of related professionals, such as lawyers, accountants, engineers, and architects, when your property is managed by an established, industry-respected larger management company.

Also, owing to their greater personnel and financial resources, larger management companies are generally more able to customize services (e.g., financial and operational procedures), to accommodate your property's unique needs.

Mid-size management companies typically manage between 30 and 80 properties. These companies may claim to offer a more personalized approach, easier access to principals and in-house professionals, and economy of scale relative to finances similar to that of a larger management company. But these companies must be able to provide service at least as good as their larger competition or you won't get your money's worth.

Depending on the age, philosophy, and level of expertise of a mid-size management company, you will find yourself working with either a slightly smaller version of a large management company, or a slightly larger version of a small management company. You'll need to use your best investigation, observation, and interview skills to determine the true value to your property of the mid-size company you're considering.

Smaller management companies typically manage between 10 and 25 properties and claim to give total personal attention to each, although they may not be able to deliver on that promise if their revenues cannot support a large enough in-house staff. Many smaller companies outsource much of their back-office work. Although some do, many smaller companies cannot provide internal special services, and do not have the years of experience or proven track record your property wants.

Very small and/or newly-created management companies, which may be operated by only a few individuals, may (or may not) offer the most personalized services, but rarely possess the back-office technology to enable them to provide the complete menu of services in-house. Very small and/or newly-created management companies also usually lack the resources to provide special services internally; they cannot offer impressive purchasing power; and they need time to develop a reputable track record.

In considering a very small and/or newly-created management company, you and your decision-making colleagues must determine how comfortable you are sitting in the middle of – and paying for – someone else's learning curve.

Generally, if the very small and/or newly-created company you're considering is owned and run by a veteran management professional, you may expect better service than you would from a company started by someone who thinks that management is an interesting way to pass the time but who hasn't done it before. Always ask for and review the credentials of the principal(s) in question.

Your biggest concern in dealing with mid-size, small, and new companies should be the impact of the firm's growth on your property's service. Poorly-planned expansion in terms of new client properties can result in your site professional/ managing agent's assignment to additional properties, which may detract from his/her ability to conscientiously attend to your property.

Additionally, the lower initial fee you may pay to a growing company will likely increase rapidly and substantially as the company requires more revenue to support its growth.

If you are contemplating hiring a growing company, be sure to ascertain from its principal(s) how the growth is being modulated and managed. Otherwise, your property may be in for disappointing surprises soon after you sign.

Under any circumstances, when your property considers a company, be it large or small, experienced or new to the field, you'll want to make certain that a seasoned management team is assigned to your property, that this team is not overloaded with too many properties, and that your property will always get the attention it needs.

Management and Your Property's Finances

While your property is foremost a residential environment, it is simultaneously a business that must operate within a budget and must be accountable to its owners. As a landlord/owner, developer/sponsor/converter, or Board member, your responsibility to your property's financial integrity is of paramount importance.

(11)

> *... make certain that a seasoned management team is assigned to your property, that this team is not overloaded with too many properties, and that your property will always get the attention it needs.*

Landlords/owners, developers/sponsors/converters, and Boards depend on professional management in varying degrees for help managing their properties' finances. In general, it is legitimate to expect your management company to:

- Collect, post, and deposit rent/maintenance/ common charge collections and all other receivables
- Record and remit payables in a timely and professional manner
- Keep track of, and pay, staff salaries
- Prepare and monitor both an operational and a long-term major capital improvement budget; and
- Honestly, accurately, and responsibly oversee your property's financial activities.

To accomplish these goals, most management companies maintain staffs of professional bookkeepers, each of whom may handle several client accounts. The company's Controller generally supervises the bookkeepers, and typically oversees both the company's internal finances and the company's financial services to its client portfolio. In many cases, the Controller is a Certified Public Accountant (CPA), which is desirable.

(12)

Generally, the most visible and quantifiable measure of a management company's ability to monitor and manage your property's finances is reflected in the Monthly Financial Statement. This is a monthly report of all financial activities within a property. The Statement should be prepared by the management company and presented timely to the property's financial decision-maker(s).

Because many property decision-makers are not themselves experts in accounting, any Monthly Financial Statement prepared by management should be appropriately detailed yet simple and accessible to read.

The Monthly Financial Statement prepared by management should:

- Include Statements of Operations (which should contain a budget analysis reconciled to your property's bank statement[s], Income, Expense, Cash Flow, and necessary Footnotes)
- Contain clearly identifiable line items and specifically dedicated categories, so that anyone can easily find information required to make educated decisions
- Be presented timely. (In the case of a Board of decision-makers, the Financial Statement should be presented several days prior to the regularly-scheduled Board meeting so members can review it and come to the meeting prepared to discuss it and ask appropriate questions about it.)

In addition to the standard monthly Financial Report, a management company also should be willing and able to provide accurate, up-to-date, and timely interim reports whenever you request them.

Furthermore, a management company also should be willing and able to provide a monthly, updated statement of arrears and sublet tracking, and should have the ability to enforce late payment and sublet fees, as well as all other internal policies established by your property.

During a management interview, many companies will promise to custom-tailor your property's Monthly Financial Report according to your instruction. Whether or not they actually will – or even have the ability to do so – is something you need to ascertain early. You can do this by asking to see sample Financial Reports, and by talking to other property decision-makers who currently employ those companies.

Generally, the most visible and quantifiable measure of a management company's ability to monitor and manage your property's finances is reflected in the Monthly Financial Statement... The Statement should be prepared and presented timely... any Monthly Financial Statement prepared by management should be appropriately detailed yet simple and accessible to read.

(14)

Some Words To The Wise ...

Never give your management company unrestricted authority to handle your property's finances.

Beware of companies that co-mingle their portfolio properties' collections, disbursements, and/or payroll accounts.

You have the right – indeed, the responsibility – to demand that the management company open bank accounts on behalf of your property only under your property's federal identification number; that you, as owner or designated Board member, share signatory rights with the management company on any or all of your property's accounts; to see original bills before they are paid; to maintain a separate account controlled only by you as the landlord/owner, developer/sponsor/converter, or Board; and to dictate to the management company special instructions for paying invoices, monitoring cash flow, making collections, and designing your Financial Statements.

It is incumbent upon you and your decision-making colleagues to question and become familiar with the system of internal checks and balances established by any management company you consider engaging.

When it comes to finances, there are no degrees of integrity. There is only absolute honesty ... or trouble.

(15)

Management Technology

The technological revolution has contributed significantly to the speed, accuracy, and professionalism with which management companies are able to service their clients. A tour of any serious management company office will reveal computers at almost every workstation, sophisticated communication devices, and a full array of cutting-edge equipment.

A truly first-rate management company recognizes the wisdom of investing in state-of-the-art technology. This up-front investment ultimately results in substantial savings of manpower and time.

Among the recent developments in management technology are the availability of on-site computer hook-ups with the central management location for immediate access to financial and other information; on-line PC hook-ups to the central management computer for designated property decision-makers (such as Treasurers who work late night hours on behalf of their properties); and interactive E-mail to expedite communication between property decision-makers and their management professionals.

Additionally, advances in management computer software now allow far more flexibility in report formatting than ever before. So it really *is* possible for many management organizations to provide custom-designed reports to their portfolio clients.

However, the existence of such flexible technology does

not guarantee that a company can or will utilize it. Therefore, you must make certain that any management company you consider employs one or more professionals with the computer expertise to execute and maintain format changes according to your needs and instructions.

Of course, just because a management company has made an investment in new technologies doesn't mean that the company provides better service. But companies that lag behind in their technological capabilities eventually will not be able to keep up with their more foresightful competition. Their techniques may be archaic and not as responsive, and they may spend more time performing tasks than actually visiting properties and taking care of business.

For the most part, visionary management companies that have read the technological writing on the wall are making a statement that they at least want to provide the fastest, most up-to-the-moment, most complete menu of services to their clients.

The technological revolution has contributed significantly to the speed, accuracy, and professionalism with which management companies are able to service their clients... A truly first-rate management company recognizes the wisdom of ... state-of-the-art technology.

TWO:

FEES AND
INTERNAL MANAGEMENT
COMPANY OPERATIONS

An interesting and sometimes baffling aspect of the professional residential management industry is the wide disparity of fees charged.

To correctly interpret the fees you will be quoted during your management search, it's helpful to understand something about the fixed internal costs of operating a management organization.

Almost universally, payroll and employee benefits account for the largest internal operating expense. After that comes standard overhead: rent, office equipment, and other normal costs of doing business.

The fact is, most management companies operate on a relatively tight profit margin.

That said, it's important for you and your decision-making colleagues to be certain that any management organization you're considering is operating profitably.

Reasonable profitability is a reflection of good internal business planning, and the pitfalls of getting involved with an unprofitable company are many.

You and your colleague decision-makers should feel comfortable asking the management companies you interview to explain how they calculated the fee they have quoted to you.

Most management companies calculate their fee quotes based at least partly on the following:

- The size and kind of property, and the number of units to be managed
- The age and condition of the property
- The length of time the property has been a rental, a co-op, condo, or townehouse/homeowners association
- Site professional/managing agent travel time to and from the property
- Results of a preliminary property walk-through prior to contract
- Special property requirements and requests.

Beware of management companies that provide firm fee quotes to you before they have visited your property and discussed its unique management needs with you. Every property is different, and you do not want to pay a fee so high that part of it goes to the management of another property within that company's portfolio. Nor do you want to pay a fee so low that it cannot support the services you need.

It is therefore wise to steer clear of management companies that quote one standard per-unit fee for all their properties, or that provide a firm quote before they have become acquainted with your property.

Regarding a management company's internal operation, you can find out how well the company is run internally by asking the following questions:

- How many properties do you service? How many total units?
- How many full- and part-time people do you employ?
- What is the average salary of your site professionals/managing agents?
- What benefits do you provide to your employees?
- What level of academic and professional education do you require of your site professionals/managing agents?
- What is the level of academic and professional education attained by the site professional/managing agent you intend to assign to our property, and what are his/her professional credentials?
- What is your formula for calculating your current fees, your fee increases, and your profit margin?
- How will you afford to manage this property without detracting from service to the other properties you manage?
- For what services not included in your service menu do you charge extra?

- What services will we lose if we negotiate a lower fee?
- Will you match the lowest management quote we get? If so, how can you do that without reducing your promised services, and which services will we lose? If not, why not?
- Are there now, or have there ever been, any claims against your company's errors and omissions policy?
- Has your company ever been, or is it now, involved in any litigation with former or present clients?

It's important ... to be certain that any management company you're considering is operating profitably... the pitfalls of getting involved with an unprofitable company are many.

As mentioned earlier, you and your decision-making colleagues will want to be wary of management companies that quote an unusually low contract fee. In many cases, this can mean hidden costs, an incomplete or reduced service menu, a lack of experience, or financial and/or operational desperation.

No matter how intriguing a very low fee quote may be, it makes better sense to question such a quote than one that may at first appear to be unusually high.

Over time, the management company you engage should be able to save your property a large part of what you pay them. In the end, lower fees can wind up costing more, and higher fees can result in a better run, more financially stable property.

The fee you pay to your management company is a real investment in your property's future. Truly good management companies are worth every penny.

Most management companies calculate their fee quotes based at least partly on the following:

- *The size and kind of property, and the number of units to be managed*
- *The age and condition of the property*
- *The length of time the property has been a rental, a c-op, a condo, or an HOA*
- *Site professional/managing agent travel time to and from the property*
- *Results of a preliminary property walk-through prior to contract*
- *Special property requirements and requests.*

THREE:

PROFESSIONALISM AND INTEGRITY IN THE MANAGEMENT ARENA

The residential property management industry has come a long way from the days when the superintendent banged on the door for the rent. Today's site professionals/managing agents are better educated and more professional than ever before. They must possess well-developed organizational, inter-personal, and time management skills to do their jobs well and to be paid commensurate with their experience, expertise, and performance.

The management industry is making noteworthy progress in standardizing practices, training and certifying personnel, and establishing an industry-wide Code of Ethics. Nevertheless, prudent decision-makers will do everything in their power to protect their properties against unscrupulous individuals and companies.

To this end, property decision-makers in increasing numbers are holding their management companies accountable for the integrity of management employees. Most property decision-makers expect, and most management companies

(25)

provide, a fidelity insurance bond covering their properties in the event of incompetence or impropriety by a site professional/managing agent.

Conscientious property decision-makers will demand that their management company either has in place, or immediately establishes, a meticulous bidding process to which all management employees must adhere.

Property decision-makers also will investigate and require from management programs of internal quality assurance.

(Computerized call accounting is one example of what is meant by internal quality assurance. Through computerized call accounting, a management company's principal[s] can monitor and keep track of every call that comes into and goes out of the office. In this way, principals can be made aware of the number of calls a site professional/managing agent receives in a given time period, as well as the sources and nature of these calls. The system also monitors and documents how quickly the site professional/managing agent responds to calls within the same time period, as well as how many calls the site professional/managing agent initiated him/herself. This last feature informs principals of whether or not their site professionals/managing agents are proactive or reactive on behalf of client properties.)

Computerized call accounting is but one system that provides quality assurance control. As you and your decision-making colleagues interview prospective companies, be sure to ask what quality assurance systems each has in place. Then compare responses for a revealing picture of what's available, who's using it, and who isn't.

In addition, decision-makers considering a change in management should conduct in-depth reference checks on the new site professional/managing agent assigned to their property; they should require disclosure statements from site professionals/managing agents and company principals regarding whether or not they accept gratuities from vendors/contractors; and they should look for companies with a clearly stated Corporate Code of Ethics, which should be explicitly included in the employment agreement of every management employee, and which every management employee must sign. (A Sample Employee Code of Ethics appears at the end of this section.)

The residential property management industry has come a long way from the days when the superintendent banged on the door for the rent... The management industry is making noteworthy progress in standardizing practices, training and certifying personnel, and establishing an industry-wide Code of Ethics. Nevertheless, prudent decision-makers will do everything in their power to protect their properties...

While the qualifications, education, credentials, and background check of a proposed site professional/managing agent are major factors in your management decision, you and your decision-making colleagues should not base your choice solely on the merits or demerits of one individual. The site professional/managing agent you like today may up and leave your property and/or the management company for any number of professional or personal reasons.

Rather, your management decision should be based on your overall favorable impression of the entire management operation.

Remember: You are hiring a whole company, not an individual.

As a property decision-maker seeking new management, you will want to bear in mind that the residential management field is rife with opportunities for poor judgment and questionable actions. You are well-advised to do your homework before you sign a contract, or your property may pay the price later.

> *... your management decision should be based on your overall favorable impression of the entire management operation. Remember: You are hiring a whole company, not an individual.*

SAMPLE EMPLOYEE CODE OF ETHICS

XYZ MANAGEMENT CORPORATION

I, _(Name of Management Company Employee)_ , understand that the terms listed below are the direct policies of my employer, XYZ Management Corporation. In the event that I violate any one of these policies, I understand that my employment with XYZ Management Corporation will be terminated immediately.

1. It is the policy of XYZ Management Corporation that no employee is allowed to receive or accept any gratuities, finders fee, or gifts of any kind from any vendor associated in any way with XYZ Management Corporation or with any property managed by XYZ Management Corporation.

2. In the event that any employee of XYZ Management Corporation is ever offered gratuity, finders fee, or any gifts from any vendor associated in any way with XYZ Management Corporation, it is that employee's obligation to notify the principals of XYZ Management Corporation of this event in writing within 24 hours.

3.	It is the policy of XYZ Management Corporation that any and all major capital improvements (jobs in excess of [specific dollar amount]) must be competitively bid. This entails sealed bids to be opened by either the property owner or a designated Board member and/or the property's engineer/architect. Under no uncertain terms is any managing agent permitted to open any bid for major capital improvements.

4.	In the event that a property owner or Board member requests advice on the selection of vendors, it is XYZ Management Corporation's policy to suggest that the owner/Board interview the vendors in question and that the owner/Board contact the vendors' references personally. The only exception to this policy is in the event that XYZ Management Corporation has experienced documented dissatisfaction with a vendor's performance.

I understand that the above policies are directly related to the terms of my employment with XYZ Management Corporation, and that both my professional reputation and the reputation of XYZ Management Corporation depend on my adherence to them.

I have read and fully understand the above.

_____ (Employee's Name) _____
_____ (Employee's Signature) _____
_____ (Date) _____
_____ (Signature of Management Principal) _____

FOUR:

WHAT TO THINK ABOUT BEFORE YOU START YOUR SEARCH

Your property's motivation for seeking new management is an important element in your search process.

Why are you in the market? Has your property's developer or sponsor recently relinquished Board control to the owners, who now want to engage an independent management entity? Are you dissatisfied with the way your current management company is performing? If so, exactly what is unsatisfactory, and how do you think it should be done better? Is your current management fee too high?

The reason you're looking for new management is a good place to start when you think about the kind of management you want.

Know Your Property

Every property has unique and specific needs in order to function optimally. Identifying your property's individual current and future requirements will help you find the management company that can best satisfy those needs.

When you examine and evaluate your property relative to its management requirements, consider these questions:

- How big is your property, and how many units does it contain?
- How old is your property, and how does its age affect the level of attention it needs?
- What special attention does your property need to its structural/buildingwide systems?
- What special physical maintenance concerns does your property have? (e.g., pool, landscaping, roof deck, etc.)
- What is your property's current and anticipated financial condition?
- What immediate and long-term capital plans are you undertaking or considering for your property?
- How well does your property's staff perform?
- What amenities does your property offer, or would your property like to offer?

This information is vital if you plan to ask the right questions during the all-important interview process.

Who Can You Count On For Help?

Some lucky communally-owned properties (co-ops, condos, HOAs) are home to many people who want to get involved. These people understand the nature of their investment, they want to know what's going on, and they are eager to contribute their time and energy to help make it the best place it can be.

Other properties reflect the real world: 80% of the work is done by 20% – or less – of the people. In these properties, a core group of dedicated individuals does most of the work that benefits everyone who lives there.

Still other properties have difficulty finding enough interested communal owners to participate on committees or take on special assignments, let alone serve on the Board.

And if you are a landlord/owner or developer/sponsor, the entire burden of operation is yours alone.

When you consider the level of management service and involvement your property needs, consider these questions:

For properties with Boards:

- How active and involved are the residents of your property?
- Do the people who own your property communally view it as an investment to be leased or sublet, or as their long-term home?
- Does your property depend on the services of outside professionals, like architects and designers, or does it use the talents of residents for such services?

(33)

- Is your Board hands-on, or does the Board set policy and delegate the responsibility for carrying it out to management?

For properties with Boards, and individually-owned properties:

- How well and how often are residents/communal owners informed of internal developments?
- Do you, or does the Board, respond to resident complaints and concerns, or will that be the responsibility of management?
- Does your property have a significant transient population?

Honest answers to these questions will let you know what level of professional management your property really needs. Then you can share this information with prospective companies so everyone knows what to expect.

Every property has unique and specific needs in order to function optimally. Identifying your property's individual current and future needs will help you find the management company that can best satisfy those needs.

FIVE:

THE SEARCH

Your First Step: Narrow The Field

When you begin your management search, your first step is to narrow the field. It would take far too much time and effort to interview every available management company, and many of them are not appropriate for your property, anyway.

Word-of-mouth recommendations and personal observation are the best ways to identify the management companies you're going to approach.

If you know people who own or live in properties that appear to be clean and well-run, ask them who their management company is. If a nearby property catches your eye, talk to the owner, a resident, the superintendent, or a doorman and find out who the management company is. Observe how many plaques from the same management companies you see as you pass neighboring properties similar to yours, then note whether or not you like the way the properties look, and why.

Do not rely on the size or frequency of advertisements to indicate a management company's size or capabilities. And for reasons of ethics and potential vested interest, don't rely on vendors or contractors to recommend a company.

On the other hand, do use the frequency with which you see positive, objective press about a company as a preliminary starting point.

And, after you have identified the companies you'd like to investigate, do pass their names by your property's outside professionals (such as legal counsel, accountants, engineers, architects, etc.). These individuals generally have experience working with several management companies in your geographical location, and for their own professional reasons, they should have your property's best interests in mind. So you may find their insights to be valuable.

Of course, don't take any reference – good or bad – at face value. (Even your property's trusted professionals may have their own unspoken reasons for referring or recommending a particular firm.) In the end, it's wisest to do your own thorough investigation for a well-rounded profile of the companies you're considering.

If, using the techniques described above, you can come up with a list of between three and five management companies to interview, you can probably find one among them that can do a good job for your property.

Your Next Step: Getting The Information You Want

Once you've identified the management companies you'd like to investigate, write a letter to the company principal on your property's stationery. Writing a letter is more desirable than calling because you don't want to get into the company's 'selling cycle' yet.

If you get into a phone conversation with a principal who knows that you're a prospective client, you may be pressured into setting up an appointment or revealing information before you are ready to move to that level. By contrast, sending a letter with clear instructions for response keeps *you* in control of the situation.

A sample request-for-information letter appears on the next page. It is composed as though it were coming from a Board, and can be changed appropriately to reflect your interest as a landlord/owner or developer/sponsor.

As you will see, this letter introduces your property and requests specific information by a stipulated deadline. Companies that fail to meet your deadline, or that contact you prematurely (except to request to do a pre-interview walk-through of your property, which is a good sign), should be eliminated immediately.

If they don't take your first instructions seriously, how will they respond later on?

SAMPLE
PRELIMINARY INFORMATION REQUEST LETTER

ZERO STREET OWNERS CORPORATION
000 ZERO STREET
ANYTOWN, ANYSTATE   00000

Date

Management Company Principal
Terrific Management, Inc.
Great Service Road
Anytown, Anystate   00000

Dear Ms./Mr. (Name of Management Company Principal):

The Board of Zero Street Owners Corporation is currently reviewing our property's management options. Zero Street Owners Corporation is a 150-unit cooperative located at Zero Street between Oak and Elm Avenues.

If you would like to present your company for our consideration, please begin the process by supplying to me, via mail, the following information:

- Your company's complete service menu, including ancillary services such as brokerage, mortgage assistance, etc.

(38)

- Information regarding your staff, including:

  * The number of properties managed by your company; the number of site professionals/managing agents in your employ; and the names and sizes of the properties managed by each site professional/managing agent

  * The backgrounds and qualifications, including but not limited to professional experience and technical expertise, of all your site professionals/managing agents, especially but not only the site professional/managing agent you would propose for our property

  * A list of all your in-house professionals, including consultants, and their qualifications

- A copy of your management agreement, and sample copies of monthly Financial Statements and other management reports

- Your in-house capability for handling rentals and tracking subleases within our property

- A list of no fewer than five existing client references, including names, Board positions, property addresses, and day and evening phone numbers

- Any other information you care to
  provide

You may send your response to me at the address above no later than (deadline date). I will contact you after I have shared your information with the Board.

Sincerely,

D. Cision-Maker

Ms. D. Cision-Maker
Vice President
Zero Street Owners Corporation

Word-of-mouth recommendations and personal observation are the best ways to identify the management companies you're going to approach... Writing a letter is more desirable than calling because you don't want to get into the company's 'selling cycle' yet... sending a letter with clear instructions for response keeps you in control of the situation ... Companies that fail to meet your deadline, or that contact you prematurely, ... should be eliminated immediately. If they don't take your first instructions seriously, how will they respond later on?

After you've gathered the requested information and checked it for thoroughness and professionalism of response, you and your decision-making colleagues should review the packages and discard those with which the majority feel uncomfortable. There may or may not be a logical, easily stated reason for this discomfort, and that doesn't matter. The right chemistry is just about as vital to a good property/management match as any service that can be offered.

The point at which you call the references supplied is up to you. Realize that the management companies are going to provide only names of properties that have expressed satisfaction with their services.

When you do decide to call the references, however, don't just ask how they like the management company. Ask also for specific information about how the management company has performed for them, and ask what they *don't* like about the management company. Filter what you hear through your own property's unique requirements.

When you've selected the management companies you want to explore further, contact the individual who responded to your written request; arrange an interview date when the company principal, the proposed site professional/managing agent, and all your property's decision-makers can attend; and set aside sufficient time to ask and get answers to all your questions.

And before you hang up, make an appointment to visit the management offices before the interview.

Touring the Management Office

You know that you can learn a lot about people by visiting their homes. The same is true of management companies.

When you tour management companies, you'll probably be accompanied by principals who will show you what they want you to see. Of course, listen to what they tell you as they lead you around. But use your eyes to gather information, as well. And take notes.

Notice where the offices are located. If it matters to you and to the management company, are the offices in reasonable proximity to your property? Is the building in which they are housed well-maintained?

Notice the appearance of the office. Is it clean and well-organized? Does the back-office appear to be busily productive? Are the people professional or slovenly in their demeanor? Is the attitude relaxed and informal, or staid and conservative, and which attitude will best serve your property?

Does the receptionist respond to telephone calls politely or curtly? How do the other employees sound on the phone? What are the site professionals/managing agents doing at their desks?

Does the equipment appear to be modern and well-maintained? Is there a meeting room that can accommodate your Board or other special meetings, if necessary?

What kind of filing system is used? Where are the principals' offices in relation to the rest of the staff? Do you get the feeling that real work is being accomplished, or is there a lot of wheel-spinning going on?

Visiting a management company's place of internal operation will enable you to formulate a more complete impression of the company. You'll know very quickly whether or not you're impressed.

Bear in mind that a luxurious office doesn't necessarily indicate efficiency any more than a spare office environment necessarily indicates low profitability.

Then, prepare for the all-important interview.

Here's a quick way to narrow the field:

Call the prospective company between 9:00 AM and 5:00 PM and see how quickly, politely, and responsively your call is taken.

Then call at 8:50 AM and 5:10 PM.

Is anybody there?

SIX:

THE INTERVIEW

When arranging your management interview schedule, you and your colleague decision-makers should determine in advance how much information you want and expect to get from each interview. You should set an individual interview time limit and inform the candidates beforehand so that they know what to expect and can prepare accordingly.

Many property decision-makers, eager to get on with the business of selecting new management, arrange all their interviews for the same evening and schedule them one after the other. The advantage to this is that all or most of your property's decision-makers are together in one place at the same time and can get and review the same information.

The disadvantage is that such a schedule may not allow you the time to explore more fully the companies you want to get to know better. Also, as with many competitive presentation situations, the first presenter is often forgotten as successive prospects make their presentations. Hence, the importance of taking detailed notes cannot be overemphasized.

When you set up the room where the interview will take place, arrange for enough seating to comfortably accommodate everyone who will be present. Provide a table and any other appropriate presentation aids for the management company representative to use, and situate your property's decision-makers so that everyone can see the representative and the representative can see them.

After introductions, the first thing that usually happens at a management interview is a presentation from the management company representative. Listen attentively to catch any discrepancies between what you've learned about the company so far and what you're being told now.

When the management company representative has finished presenting, it's your turn to ask questions. This is the most important part of the interview. When the curtain goes up, you'll be both audience and player. Make sure you know what to say.

To that end, here's a checklist of the most important questions you and your colleague decision-makers can feel comfortable asking at the interview. Many questions and answers will be repeats of information you have already solicited; listen carefully for additional information and response discrepancies.

Remember: Choosing a management company is an important decision. You have the right to have your questions answered honestly, completely, and up front.

The 40 Most Important Questions To Ask

1. Why are you interested in managing our property?

2. Is your company set up to provide all the services listed on pages 5 and 6 of this book?

3. What additional services does you company provide, and what are the charges for them?

4. How many properties does your company manage?

5. How many properties has your company added in the last year, and how did you get the business? (e.g., solicitation, word-of-mouth, merger/acquisition, etc.)

6. How many properties are managed by the site professional/managing agent you propose for our property?

7. How big are the other properties managed by the proposed site professional/managing agent, and how will this person fit our property into his/her schedule?

8. What are the academic and professional education, training, certification, and experience backgrounds of the site professional/managing agent you are proposing for our property?

(47)

9. How long has your proposed site professional/ managing agent been with your company?

10. How can we go about getting a background check on your proposed site professional/managing agent?

11. What type of in-house support and administrative assistance will our site professional/managing agent get to service our property?

12. How many other site professionals/managing agents are on staff, and how will our site professional/ managing agent's vacation and sick days impact our property?

13. What role will our site professional/managing agent play in our monthly meetings?

14. Can we expect a written monthly Management Report at every regularly scheduled monthly meeting?

15. What type of benefits package do you provide to your site professionals/managing agents, and what type of 'perks' do they get?

16. Who in your organization is ultimately responsible for our site professional/managing agent's performance?

17. What is the procedure for requesting a replacement site professional/managing agent if we are dissatisfied with his/her performance?

18. Who will be responsible for overseeing our property's finances?

19. Who oversees your company's bookkeeping?

20. Is your Controller a CPA?

21. Will you format monthly Financial Statements according to our instruction, or are all your reports uniform?

22. Who owns your company?

23. What are the management background and experience of your company's principal(s)?

24. Is your company's owner present in the office on a regular basis, and how accessible is s/he to your clients?

25. Will you provide to us the home phone numbers of our site professional/managing agent and your company's principal(s)?

26. How can we contact our site professional/managing agent and/or your company's principal(s) in the event of an emergency?

27. What is your emergency procedure?

28. What is your company's purchasing policy and procedure for tracking and stocking supplies?

29. What is your company's major project bidding procedure?

30. What quality assurance programs do you have in place?

31. What type of fidelity bond do you offer for our property's protection?

32. How did you calculate the fee you are requesting?

33. What services are not included in the fee quoted? Why aren't these services included, and how much extra do you charge to provide them?

34. What services will we lose if we negotiate a lower fee?

35. Will you match the lowest quote we get? If so, how can you do that without reducing your promised services, and which services will we lose? If not, why not?

36. How do you calculate your fee increases, and how often do you request them?

37. How do you measure, track, and document client satisfaction?

38. Is there an 'escape clause' in your management contract?

39. **Will you work with us on a six-month probationary basis?**

40. **Who are your major competitors, and how do you differ from them?**

Here are some good ways to get the management company representative talking, and to find out information you otherwise might not get:

• Review local residential management industry publications and the real estate section of your local newspaper to find a company's advertisements. Bring one or two of their ads to the interview and point out claims that are made in the ads. Ask how those services work and how the company intends to implement them for your property. Ask if the company will make those services a stipulated part of your management contract, if they aren't already.

• Relate a situation in which you were dissatisfied with your existing or previous management company's performance. Explain the situation to the management company representative but don't say how the other management company handled it. Ask how the prospective management company would respond.

• If it hasn't already been done, ask the management company representative to arrange for a walk-through of your property, a meeting with your staff, and a written report of observations and recommendations.

(51)

• Contact local real estate organizations that accredit industry professionals and ask which companies are actively involved in enhancing the professional education of their site professionals/managing agents and support staff.

After introductions, the first thing that usually happens at a management interview is a presentation from the management company representative. Listen attentively to catch any discrepancies between what you've learned about the company so far and what you're being told now.

When the management company representative has finished presenting, it's your turn to ask questions. This is the most important part of the interview. Make sure you know what to say.

SEVEN:

THE CONTRACT

Okay. You and your colleague decision-makers have selected the management company you would like to engage, and have informed that company of your decision.

Your next step is to direct the principal of your chosen management company to submit a copy of their proposed contract to you and your decision-making colleagues, and to your property's legal counsel for review.

You will find that, for the most part, contracts for your type of property are pretty standard, with boiler-plate legalese and blanks to be filled in with information specific to your property.

While it would be nice to believe that a handshake on verbally agreed-to terms and conditions would suffice, prudent business demands that everything be in writing. You will want certain specific terms and conditions to be clearly stated in the contract in order to avoid future misunderstandings and potential unpleasantry.

(53)

Specific Contract Terms and Conditions

- ### *Areas of Responsibility*

  The contract should define as clearly as possible all areas
  of responsibility for the management company and the
  site professional/managing agent. These areas of
  responsibility should include but may not be limited
  to: financial; operational; long-term planning; and
  labor and owner/resident/tenant relations.

- ### *Property Staff Supervision*

  The contract should clearly indicate that, while your
  property's employees report directly to the designated
  site professional/managing agent, they are nevertheless
  employed by your property. Therefore, the contract must
  clearly state that the site professional/managing agent
  must seek and get approval from your property's
  decision-makers before hiring or firing any individual
  in your property's employ; must maintain accurate and
  up-to-date employee records to be shared with your
  property's decision-makers; and must inform your
  property's decision-makers in a timely manner of
  any labor-related problems or disputes as they arise.

- *Performance Indemnification and Management Company Insurance*

  The contract should indicate a clearly stated indemnification clause, which stipulates that the site professional/ managing agent assigned to your property shall be held to the standard of negligence. If the management company insists on being held to the standard of gross negligence, which allows greater latitude for inappropriate or inadequate services, beware.

  In addition, the contract should clearly require the management organization and site professional/ managing agent to maintain the following insurance coverage: errors and omissions; fidelity bond; and general liability. Limits must be adequate and appropriate to your property. (Consult your property's individual insurance carrier to determine the appropriate limits for this condition.) A copy of endorsements and/or a letter from the management company's insurance carrier should be annexed to the contract.

- *Hours of Operation*

  The standard hours of operation of the management company's primary location should be clearly stated within the contract. In addition, a list of holidays during which the management company will be closed also should be included.

- ***Emergency Response***

  The contract should include a clause whereby the management company indicates their willingness, ability, and intention to make available to your property either your assigned site professional/managing agent or a company principal in the event of an emergency within your property. In addition, the contract should clearly explain the management company's emergency procedures, including those established to address emergencies that occur outside the company's standard hours of operation.

- ***Contract Cancellation/Expiration***

  The Cancellation of Service clause in the contract should be clear and precise. The contract should not be written to assume automatic renewal. The contract should stipulate that it is the responsibility of the management company to inform your property's decision-makers in writing in a timely manner in advance of the contract's stipulated expiration date.

- ***Attorney's Review Including Documents***

  Your property's legal counsel should review the proposed contract and revise it appropriately before your property makes a commitment to a new management organization. Your property's legal counsel (who, in this case, should be an independent legal counsel and not a Board member who happens to be a lawyer), should review the entire proposed contract, including the following documents, which should be supplied by the management company and annexed to the contract: Purchasing Policy, Code of Ethics, and Corporate Hiring Policy.

- ***Transition Considerations***

    The contract should contain a clearly defined outline of how your new management company intends to effect a smooth management transition.

... prudent business demands that everything be in writing. You will want certain specific terms and conditions to be clearly stated in the contract in order to avoid future misunderstandings and potential unpleasantry ...

EIGHT:

THE TRANSITION

Congratulations. Your property has engaged a new management company and, in a perfect world, everything should proceed smoothly.

Unfortunately, that's not always how it works in the real world. Often, properties in transition find themselves in a kind of management limbo: no longer receiving total attention from the outgoing management company, and not yet fully integrated into the systems of the new management company.

Your property may find your outgoing management company slow to respond to your requests or the requests of your new management company for vital information or documents. You may find your new management company slow to implement all of the operational aspects you had requested and they had promised. Your property's staff may be slow to acclimate to a change in supervision. And your property's residents may be confused by changes in procedure and personnel.

Because the first month of transition is the most challenging for both a property and its new management, some companies will begin the transition process, including communicating with the outgoing management company, 30 days before their contract start date and at no charge to your property. During this time, and until the transition has been successfully accomplished, it is particularly crucial for you and your decision-making colleagues to stay on top of things.

Even with cooperation from the management firm you are replacing, you and your decision-making colleagues need to personally ensure that certain important files, documents, and information are immediately accessible to your new management company.

These include but are not limited to your property's:

- Multiple Dwelling Registration Cards
- 1098 Tax Information
- Mortgage and Tax Payment Schedules
- Rent rolls and tenant lists
- Outstanding resident arrearages
- Outstanding violations
- All existing contracts and warranties/guarantees from vendors/contractors
- All documents regarding your property's relationship with outside professionals (e.g., legal counsel, accountants, etc.)
- Individual property labor agreements
- Outstanding payables
- Banking and investment account information

- Outstanding resident complaints/work requests
- Minutes book
- All other documents pertaining to your property's ongoing operation.

You can expect your outgoing management organization to insist on retaining a Contingency Fund to cover residual expenses related to your property after you have gone to another management firm. This is reasonable up to one month, after which you should demand an accounting of funds disbursed during that time, and immediate return of the remainder of the fund.

Understandably, your new management company will need time to input the appropriate data about your property into its computer system, to get used to working with your staff and residents, and to accommodate the service agreements you made during contract negotiations. You and your decision-making colleagues should be personally involved in this process, and insist that the services you contracted for be delivered timely.

Additionally, you will want to pay special attention to the way in which the transition is handled relative to two important groups: your staff, and your property's residents.

As soon as your property engages a new management company and is satisfied with the assigned site professional/ managing agent, a special staff meeting should be arranged. In attendance should be yourself if you are a landlord/owner or developer/sponsor, or a knowledgeable Board member who gets along with your property's superintendent and staff in the case

(61)

of co-ops, condos, and HOAs; your new site professional/ managing agent; and all property staff members.

Either you or a designated Board member should personally and patiently inform staff of the change in management, and explain that, while existing policies still prevail, there will probably be a change in the style of management and supervision. Staff and the new site professional/ managing agent should be allowed time to get acquainted so that an environment of mutual respect can be established.

Remember: Even the best management company cannot perform its responsibilities without the cooperation of your property's staff. And vice versa.

As for your property's residents, it is appropriate to inform them of the change in management in a timely and informational letter. This letter should introduce the new management company, explain why it was chosen, introduce the name and qualifications of the new site professional/managing agent, and provide all appropriate telephone numbers, addresses, and contact information.

Residents should be informed if there is any change in resident/management communication procedures, and of how they can communicate complaints or concerns about the new management situation to the landlord/owner, developer/sponsor, or Board.

Although as a landlord/owner or developer/sponsor, you own your property, and although as a Board you and your decision-making colleagues have been entrusted with operating your property, it is still home to the individuals who live there. And in the case of co-ops, condos, and HOAs, it represents a significant investment for those individuals, as well. Your property's residents and communal owners have a right to know what's going on in terms of management, and it is your responsibility to tell them.

... you need to personally ensure that ... important files, documents, and information are immediately accessible to your new management firm... pay special attention to the way in which the transition is handled relative to ... staff and ... residents. As soon as your property engages a new management company ..., a special staff meeting should be arranged ... Either you or a designated Board member should ... inform staff of the change in management, and explain that ... there will probably be a change in the style of management and supervision ... Residents should be informed if there is any change in resident/ management communication procedures, and of how they can communicate complaints or concerns about the new management situation ...

NINE:

A WORD ABOUT SELF-MANAGEMENT

Perhaps you and your colleague decision-makers are contemplating self-management for your property; that is, running the property yourselves without the assistance of, or with minimal assistance from, outside professional resources.

The degrees of self-management run the gamut from totally self-contained management (doing it all yourself), to engaging the 'a la carte' services of specialists in the areas where you may need them (e.g., payroll services, labor consulting, etc.), to hiring a single outside individual to oversee your property's management and answer directly and exclusively to your property's decision-maker(s).

Regardless of where your property falls along this spectrum, it's important to remember that the management of your property is a full-time job. So, while self-management may at first appear to be an interesting and potentially viable option, it is incumbent upon you and your colleague decision-makers to become thoroughly familiar with every aspect of this considerable undertaking before forging ahead.

Although there are notable exceptions, self-management is generally appropriate only for smaller properties, which may not be able to afford the fees of full-service management companies; or for financially-stable properties where all systems and procedures are operational, staff is adequate in number and performing optimally, the property's physical structure is sound, there are no major outstanding legal issues, and residents are living together harmoniously.

Even if your property meets these criteria, the most important – and challenging – aspect of self-management is finding and maintaining a dedicated group of individuals who are willing to educate themselves in every aspect of property operations (such as the technical operation of boilers, staff supervision and local labor laws, collections and payables, computer operation, and much, much more); who are willing and able to work long hours; who can put vested interests aside and work together harmoniously and productively; and who are willing to shoulder the burden of responsibility.

You and your colleague decision-makers should take a long, hard look at your property's needs compared to its financial, technical, and human resources before making the decision to self-manage. If self-management appears to be the answer for your property, then by all means, move forward.

And if self-management turns out *not* to be appropriate for your property, take heart. With a little work, you and your colleague decision-makers will surely find a professional management company that is.

TEN:

FOR MORE INFORMATION

There are a number of well-established, reputable organizations and groups on both the national and local levels that can provide more information about virtually every aspect of multi-unit residential operations. Many of them are listed below. Your phone directory can supply updated addresses and phone numbers based on the information here.

You may also want to subscribe to the *Residential Property Decision-Maker's Newsletter*. This cost-effective monthly resource provides timely, practical, and objective information on issues impacting the multi-unit residential community and your role as a residential property decision-maker. A subscription form appears on page 85 of this book.

National Information Resources

Center for Cooperative Housing
Alexandria, Virginia

Community Associates Institute
Alexandria, Virginia
(56 chapters nationwide, organized according to geographic region. Especially useful for townehouse/homeowners associations.)

Institute of Real Estate Management
Chicago, Illinois

National Association of Housing Cooperatives
Alexandria, Virginia

National Association of Realtors
Washington, D.C.

Local Information Resources

California Association of Housing Cooperatives
San Francisco, California

Cooperative and Condominium Council of Westchester
White Plains, New York

Cooperative Council of Long Island
Long Island, New York

Coordinating Council of Cooperatives
New York, New York

Council of New York Cooperatives
New York, New York

Eastern Cooperative Housing Council
Greenbelt, Maryland

Federation of New York Housing Cooperatives
New York, New York

Midwest Association of Housing Cooperatives
Taylor, Michigan

Mitchell-Lama Council
New York, New York

New Jersey Federation of Housing Cooperatives
Newark, New Jersey

Northeast Federation of Housing Cooperatives
Boston, Massachusetts

Potomac Association of Housing Cooperatives
Baltimore, Maryland

Southeast Association of Housing Cooperatives
Atlanta, Georgia

TO ORDER ADDITIONAL COPIES OF THIS BOOK, AND/OR TO SUBSCRIBE TO THE INFORMATIVE RESIDENTIAL PROPERTY DECISION-MAKER'S NEWSLETTER, SEE PAGE 85.

INDEX

C

Capital project budget/planning, 6, 12, 32
Cash flow (property), 13, 15
  monitoring, 15
  report in Monthly Financial
    Statement, 13
Categories, 13
  in Monthly Financial Statement, 13
Certified Public Accountant
  (See Controller)
Checks and balances, 15
  management co. internal, 15
Code of Ethics, 25, 27, 29-30, 57
  corporate, 27
  in contract, 57
  management industry, 25
  Sample Employee, 29-30
Codes, 3
  (See also Laws & Regulations)
Collection(s), 5, 12, 15
  co-mingling of, 15
  making, 15
  maintenance/common charges/
    rent, 5, 12
  receivables, 12
Co-mingling, 15
  of funds by management co., 15
Common charges
  collection of, 3, 5, 12
Communication, 16
  between property and management
    office, 16
  E-mail, 16
  technology, 16
Computerized call accounting, 26
Computers, 16,17

hook-ups between property &
  management office, 16
management co. in-house
  experts, 17
management technology, 16
PC hook-ups to central
  management location, 16
Condition, 20
  of property relative to fee, 20
Condo(miniums), 3, 20, 32, 62, 63
Contingency fund, 61
  during transition, 61
Contract, 5-7, 22, 28, 51, 53-57
  additional management services, 6
  basic management services, 4-6
  before signing, 28
  negotiation by management co.
    on behalf of property, 5
  procedure for review before
    signing, 49
  walk-through prior to, 20
  Inclusion of
    automatic renewal clause, 56
    copy of endorsements, 55
    Corp. Code of Ethics, 57
    Corp. Hiring Policy, 57
    indemnification clause, 55
    insurance coverages, 55
    letter from insurance carrier, 55
    list of holidays and business
      closings, 55
  Specific terms and conditions: 54-
57
    areas of management
      responsibility, 54
    attorney's review, 56
    contract cancellation, 56
    company insurance, 55

F

G

H

I

M

Maintenance, of property, 5, 32
  ongoing, 5
  preventive, 5
  special concerns, 32
Maintenance Charges, 3, 5, 12
  collection of, 3, 5, 12
Management Company, 7-11, 16-17, 19-23, 25-30, 35-61
(See also Services)
  accountability for employees, 25
  advertisements, 36, 51
  appearance of offices, 42-43
  attitude of, 42
  bidding process, 26
  choice of, 28
  contract, 53-57
    areas of responsibility, 54
    Code of Ethics, 57
    contract cancellation, 56
    emergency response, 56
    errors & omissions coverage, 55
    general liability, 55
    hiring policy, 57
    hours of operation, 55
    insurance, 55
    performance indemnification, 55
    property staff supervision, 54
    purchasing policy, 57
    standard of gross negligence, 55
    standard of negligence, 55
    transition considerations, 57
  disclosure statement, 27
  equipment, 16, 42
  fidelity insurance bond, 25-26, 55
  filing system, 43
  impression of, 43
  initial staff meeting and report, 51
  interviewing, 45-52

  location of, 20, 42
  location of principal's office, 43
  meeting room, 42
  presentation at interview, 46
  quality assurance, 26-27
  response to interview questions, 42, 51-52
  response to request for
    information, 37
  size of, 7-11
  touring offices, 16, 42-43
  internal operation, 19-23
    employee benefits, 19
    fixed internal expenses, 19
    office equipment, 16, 42
    payroll, 19
    rent, 19
  profit margin, 19
  value relative to fee, 23
  walk-through of property and
    report, 20, 37, 51
Management industry, 25
  Code of Ethics, 25
  personnel certification, 25
  personnel training, 25
  standardizing practices, 25
Management team, 11
  assignment of seasoned team
    to property, 11
  workload, 11
Managing Agent (See Site
  Professional/Managing Agent)
Meeting room, at management
  office, 42
Meetings, 6, 13, 42
  at management co. office, 42
  Board meetings, 6
    regular, management attendance, 6
    special, management attendance, 6

(76)

(78)

(81)

ABOUT THE AUTHORS

LESLIE KAMINOFF, RAM, NYARM, is founder and CEO of AKAM ASSOCIATES, Inc., a full-service residential property management organization serving the metropolitan New York multi-unit dwelling community. The company has headquarters in New York City and Westchester, New York.

Kaminoff's long-time service to the real estate industry began with positions as managing agent for several New York-based commercial and residential management organizations. Immediately prior to establishing AKAM ASSOCIATES, Inc. in 1983, Kaminoff was Director of Property Management and Assistant Director of Real Estate for Mount Sinai Medical Center in New York City, where he stewarded the development of housing for hospital staff and the acquisition of real estate for hospital use.

An active participant in industry associations, Kaminoff is a member in good standing of the Associated Builders and Owners of Greater New York; the New York Association of Realty Managers; and the Rent Stabilization Association. He has served on the Board of Governors of the New York Chapter of Registered Apartment Managers, and is currently a Director of the New York Association of Realty Managers. Kaminoff holds professional certification from both the Real Estate Board of New York and the New York Association of Realty Managers.

As a well-respected member of the professional residential property management industry, Kaminoff is author of numerous articles on real estate-related topics, and is a popular and

(83)

sought-after speaker at industry seminars and conferences.

In addition to overseeing the activities of AKAM ASSOCIATES, Inc., and providing leadership to the professional property management field, Kaminoff is also an Instructor in New York University's Real Estate Institute Certification Program. He is currently working with NYU to develop and implement an internship program for professional property mangers, and a certification program in professional residential management ethics.

Leslie Kaminoff lives with his wife and their three children in Westchester, New York.

BARBARA DERSHOWITZ is an award-winning writer, and president of the Business Communications Workshop and B. Dershowitz Communications, Inc.

Dershowitz, who has served as Contributing Editor to *Real Estate Forum, Better Buildings*, and *The New York Cooperator*, is a long-time consultant to the metropolitan New York real estate industry, providing all types of communication-related services to both management and other real estate-related industries, as well as to individual co-ops and condos throughout the region. She is also the author of a series of educational skillbooks, and of the book, *The Affluent Spirit: Lessons in Spiritual and Material Abundance.*

Barbara Dershowitz lives with her husband and their two children on Long Island, New York.

SPECIAL OFFERS FOR
RESIDENTIAL PROPERTY DECISION-MAKERS

Need More Copies of *How to Choose The Right Management Company for Your Residential Property?*

YES! Please send me:

Number of books (____) at $14.95 per copy	$	_____
Shipping and handling at $3.00 per copy	$	_____
SUBTOTAL	$	_____
NY/NJ/Conn. orders add 8.5% Sales Tax	$	_____
TOTAL BOOK ORDER AMOUNT	$	_____

The Residential Property Decision-Maker's Newsletter

Delivered monthly right to your mailbox: Timely, practical, objective information you can't get anywhere else. Expertly covers issues impacting the multi-unit residential community and your role as a residential property decision-maker. $60/year.

__ YES! Activate my subscription. I've included the cost in the enclosed check.

Name _____

Address _____

City _____ State _____ Zip _____

County _____ Phone: (___) _____

Property type: Rental __   Co-op __   Condo __   HOA __

Your Decision-Making Position _____

I learned about this book/newsletter from: _____

Please mail this form, or a copy, with a check payable to: bdci, 423 Jericho Turnpike, Suite 136, Syosset, NY 11791. Allow 4-6 weeks for delivery. Thank you for your order.